PERFECTLY
Imperfect

POEMS OF ENCOURAGEMENT, REFLECTION
AND REVELATION OF GOD'S LOVE

DENISE SUTTON

Denise Sutton
Brooklyn, New York

Copyright © 2019 Denise Sutton. All rights reserved. No part of this publication may be reproduced, stored in or introduced into a retrieval system, or transmitted, in any form or by any means (electronic, mechanical, photocopying, recording or otherwise), without the prior written permission of the copyright owner.

The scanning, uploading, and distribution of this book via the Internet or any other means without the permission of the publisher are illegal and punishable by law. Please purchase only authorized electronic editions and do not participate in or encourage electronic piracy of copyrighted materials. Your support of the author's rights is appreciated.

Limits of Liability ~ Disclaimer
The author and publisher shall not be liable for your misuse of this material. This book is strictly for expressive purposes. The author and publisher shall have neither liability nor responsibility to anyone concerning any loss or damage caused, or alleged to be caused, directly or indirectly by the information contained in this book.

Cover Design: Beverly Brister, Beverly's Webshop
Editing-Interior Layout: The Self-Publishing Maven
Formatting: Istvan Szabo, Ifj. (Fiverr/Sapphire Guardian Intl.)

ISBN: 978-1-7341742-0-5

Printed in the United States of America

ACKNOWLEDGMENTS

I must acknowledge those in my life who have supported, corrected, inspired and challenged me on so many levels in this birthing process. Labor is not easy and does not feel good at all, yet the process is necessary to facilitate growth, maturity and understanding. This labor of love could not have come forth without special people who acted as doctors, nurses and health care facilitators during the process of birth.

Lord God, you are my EVERYTHING! I could not have done this work without you impregnating me with purpose!

Mommy and Granny, God gave you both special tasks to impart into me. I am so happy you completed your tasks and now I must live out my God ordained assignment with His grace and mercy leading the way. I love and miss you both so much. Not a week goes by without a thought or expression entering my treasured memory bank.

I could not have completed this project without listening and learning from Bishop Horace C. Michael and Lady Tania Michael. I know it has not been easy, but I thank you for being an example of a soldier on the front line in God's army. Your prayers, encouragement and correction were necessary and appreciated.

Teekwa Scarborough and Candida Young – SISTERS, you have pushed, encouraged and made me accountable to complete the work God started in me. Times when I retreated into that space of familiarity and allowed excuses to take place, you grabbed my hand and said, "GET TO WORK"!

Robin Devonish, I must say "thank you." I appreciate you and your gifts! You are a woman who takes care of her business and does it with style, class and grace. Thank you for being real and helping in this process of book publishing. You are "the" "SELF-PUBLISHING MAVEN" and I thank God for using you in my life through this project process!

DEDICATION

This book is dedicated to every person who has struggled with SELF.

Self-esteem, self-confidence, self-doubt and fear. You are not what the enemy or this world or even YOU label you. Once we surrender to God, SELF will die! We are God's beautiful masterpiece with gifts and talents to use for His Glory! Embrace the process of blossoming into a precious gem.

NEVER FORGET, YOU ARE A WINNER AND AN OVERCOMER!

"For I know the thoughts that I think toward you, saith the Lord, thoughts of peace, and not evil, to give you an expected end." – Jeremiah 29:11

PREFACE

I Love Jesus! God inspired each word of this book. There were many moments of laughter, worship, praying, crying and reflection during the process of this series of poems. I poured out of my heart what the Lord wanted released. It's so important to allow God to do the work in us. Everything we endure in life is for our growth. Similar to the crushing of the olive to extract the precious oil or the irritant entering an oyster to stimulate activity to form a beautiful pearl, we must go through crushing and deal with irritants in the procedure to become the righteous children of God.

I hope these poems will help and inspire you to utilize the gifts God has placed in you. No matter the circumstance or hesitation, I challenge you to press. There is greatness in our imperfect selves and God wants to use our imperfection to point to The One who is perfect, Omni present, omniscient, all knowing, wise and true. God is real! He loves us so much and we are here to love Him and others.

Lord, this is my love letter to you in poetic form.

Love, Denise

CONTENTS

Chapter I: Spirit, Soul, and Body 1
  "Flawed" 2
  "Flesh" 3
  "Church Hurt" 4
  "Surrender, Honor, Respect Rehab" 6
  "I Am A Kept Woman" 8

Chapter II: Family Love 9
  "Ma" 10
  "A Grandmother's Love" 12
  "A Charge To Keep I Have And A God To Glorify" 15

Chapter III: Freedom 17
  "Purpose" 18
  "Help" 20
  "Rise Up Lioness" 22
  "An Ode To My King" 23

CHAPTER I
SPIRIT, SOUL, AND BODY

"FLAWED"

I have learned through tests and trials
No human can profess perfection, and no one is an isle
Even though as humans we are flawed, God still wants to use us
Will you answer the call?
When you know what is right and still do wrong, do you hang your head in shame, beat yourself and crawl?
Or do you acknowledge your wrong, humble yourself before God, ask for forgiveness – you don't have to fall
Pray for restoration forgiveness and strength
We are imperfect beings striving for perfection to win
God uses imperfect people to accomplish his tasks so we can live again
You see, He is the perfect one for humankind to look up unto and adore
God is our everything. He is the source!
He perfects us, provides our resources, yet we must-
Die To self-daily.
Oh, I know it can seem hard!
However, we must remember we serve a perfect God and we are flawed

"FLESH"

Die flesh, die!
You have to go
Kill it, kill it right now!
There is no room for you to grow
You try to get the best of me
You are nothing but misery. You turn everything into a lie
Wretched flesh, YOU MUST DIE!
You are evicted! Goodbye!
Good riddance don't even come near.
Your time is up! The Holy Spirit resides in here!
Pray, fast, read. Read, fast and pray
Guess what flesh, I am not dismayed
I am growing in the spirit realm and you are becoming weak…
Day by day, I told you flesh! You can't stay!
God gave me the victory!
I declare the decree
I AM FREE!
Oh, and if you didn't catch it the first time, I will repeat it in French
J'ai la victoire et je suis libre!
Oui!

"CHURCH HURT"

Church hurt
Oh yes, it is real
Church hurt
So, what is the big deal?
We walk around angry, frustrated, bitter and sad
Our emotions are topsy turvey and you feel like you are going mad
Misunderstandings
Lack of communication
Confusion ensues
We open ourselves up to evil devices of attack
STOP
WAIT
PUMP YOUR BREAKS
God has a solution for that!
It is time to get on your knees.
Ask the Lord, Father help me please!
"Lord, help me with all of this stress.
I have made a big mistake, I repent to you
Please Father God; get me out of this mess."
Hear my humble cry, I know I do not understand why…
All the in's and out's
I bow before you Lord. Please do not let me fall

I need you; I love you and that is all
Church hurt is real
Yet God shows us how to deal
Hurt, confusion and doubt
Trust in the Lord, He will surely pull you out
The peace of God let it take root in you.
Trust in God and His word, guess what, you are on the right track boo!

"SURRENDER, HONOR, RESPECT REHAB"

No, you do not have the right to address me or any
woman as a "b", trick or whore.
I am a woman of God, show me respect or keep it
moving right out the door!
Yes, even Rehab the harlot was treated
with dignity and adored
Rehab was courageous, brave and willing to give her all.
She acknowledged her truth
At the right time, she answered the call.
She helped the spies; she had enough faith to believe,
in the one true and living God, the one that redeems.
Who forgives us of all our trespasses and heals us
from all disease. The one who sticks closer to us than
a brother, the giver of everlasting life, Elohim!
Rehab yearned to turn her life around before it was
too late. She knew if she did not submit to God's will
she and her family's earthly and eternal lives were at stake.
There are other women in the bible who were great
examples of warriors and strength. They obeyed
God's instructions and were faithful to the end. God
blessed them in their process and expanded their length
God will lengthen our days; give us peace, joy, grace
and His everlasting love.

We must know our worth and never accept less than what our Father has promised from above

The lives of Deborah, Ruth, Anna, Priscilla, and many more, ministered to the masses as they looked to their Lord for comfort,

the Holy One they adore.

Rehab was imperfect, as we all are in every way.

She spoke manifestation into her situation, "no matter what, come what may"

I must save the family and myself, I hear you Lord, and I will obey

What we must learn from Rehab's story was the beginning mistakes of her life turned around as she made the ultimate act of surrendering to the will of God through her sacrifice

"I AM A KEPT WOMAN"

I am a kept woman – Through and through
I am a kept woman – How about you?
I am a kept woman – Didn't you know?
I am a kept woman – That's right! My heavenly Father told me so!
When He formed the heavens and earth, His word tells me He created me with worth!
I am peculiar, royalty, and is forever on His mind.
I am Holy, sanctified and set apart for Him to use.
I am a kept woman – No, I Am Not To Be Abused!
I am the apple of my Fathers eye
The one He knew before my mother conceived
I am a kept woman – Yes, my Master is pleased!
I am a kept woman – Because I Believe
I AM A KEPT WOMAN OF GOD!

CHAPTER II
FAMILY LOVE

"MA"

Ma, why did you have to leave me?
Did you really have to go?
If you really wanted to stay with me, why didn't you tell me so.
Tell me what was really going on, how you were truly feeling – make it real raw, gritty and plain
Instead, we had to find out the real deal when you were so far gone in pain.
We had to watch you suffer. Listen to your countless yells and screams of agony and torture
Mommy, you had dreams
Dreams for your daughter's futures
and hopes to live long
I miss you so much mommy, I long to hear your song
Your song was filled with emotion, sometimes silence or a faint knowing look and stare
We loved you in every melody; every inaudible sound because we knew you cared
You loved your children, family and friends
And we loved you back, oh yes, we did.
Lupus may have killed your body and taken you out of this world, but I know a God who says He loves you.

He is concerned about us and He cares. God tells us
He will never leave nor forsake us. He knows our
beginning to the end

Thank you mommy for showing us love, for shaping
and molding us into the women we are. We know
you are away from us naturally and
we long to see you afar.

In our heavenly home where no pain and suffering
and heartache exists

Until that day, we remember what you taught us, we
look at your pictures and hear your voice through our
own actions, our lives, our inaudible sounds and
expressions of love toward others.

Mommy you are so profound

Please remember we love you, and I will always be
Rhetta's child

"A GRANDMOTHER'S LOVE"

Just the sound of your cackling and somewhat mischievous laughter
The secret whispers between you and your closest family and friends makes me wonder what you were seeking after
What treasure did you hold on to that only a select few could engage in? I often wonder my granny, was there something very special and completely hidden
You would say, "I thank the Lord a whole heap of times" in your old southern country voice, which to me was so refined. Granny, to me you will always appear dignified!
Yes, it is true, you did not have a high school education; you did not have a fancy title or wanted to be something you were not. Moreover, what I love the most is you did not give all that other stuff a second thought
You were just happy to be Ms. Cat.
Society may have labeled you an uneducated black teenaged dropout mother who would always be poor with a sad end, but God viewed you so differently that the world could never comprehend!
Granny, you had many victories, and I could never forget the many souls you blessed.

You went above and beyond to help those that had no place to lay their head. Some folks had no food or clothes, yet God pressed it on your heart repeatedly not to leave them for dead

You allowed God's special gift in you to stir up and selflessly offered shelter, food and a comforting word or hug. Many people have testified of your efforts and of your many acts of love

You were the one everyone flocked to and so many people loved the way you made food, cake and pies. You were the one folks felt comfortable enough to share their most intimate and sometimes tragic stories and yes, their biggest lies.

Your stories were legendary to me, oh how I miss you granny!

You may not have known it, but you are part of my destiny.

You imparted so much wisdom, lessons of how to love the unlovable and how to care.

Disrespectful greetings to my elders, oh I would never dare!

You taught me how to cook and care for others and to treat people with respect. Granny you had a way of gathering people together, you were the glue that always connect

Everyone has special memories of their grandmothers, just like the great Muhammad Ali. It is the treasures we must hold on to, the pearls of wisdom, and nuggets of strength that fills us with so much glee!

If your grandmother is with you, love on her, forgive others and let go!

Gods' ways are always right, and He makes grandmothers to help the young 'ins grow!

"A CHARGE TO KEEP I HAVE AND A GOD TO GLORIFY"

A CHARGE TO KEEP I HAVE AND A GOD TO GLORIFY
These were the words uttered from my grandmother's mouth to my ears
I asked her to repeat them again just to make sure I was clear
Clear in my mind
Clear in my understanding
Clear to write the words down with paper and pen
Clear to receive interpretation from that still small voice within
Granny Sally's voice trembling with fear and trepidation repeated those very words again…
I knew the Lord was talking to her, I knew He was giving her instruction, I knew it was only from Him
Now my granny is gone. She completed her course and time has moved on
I now hear the voice of the Holy Ghost instructing me, the time is now, no time to dilly dally
Pick up your cross, when your load seems too heavy to bear, I am right there to help you just as I did for Sally
You must pick up the torch and carry on.
Move forward my child, time to press on

You have a charge to keep and a God to glorify, I
have opened the doors and it is solidified
My child I have a mission for you to complete, but it
is not for your glory, IT IS ALL FOR ME
I AM THE CREATER, MASTER
AND KING OF KINGS!
THERE IS NO ONE BEFORE ME
OH NO, NOT A LIVING THING

CHAPTER III
FREEDOM

"PURPOSE"

Walk in purpose child
You have no time to waste
The enemy maybe chasing you, but hey, no worries…
The Lord is on that case
He loves you and is defending you each step you take
He has a plan of action to give to you
Get up and complete your race
GOD'S word says the race is not to the swift nor the battle to the strong, neither yet bread to the wise…yes, and the verse continues.
We must stay on track. Keep up the pace.
People are waiting on you to guide them to the perfect place
The place where God dwells, where He communes with us and sets us straight
Straight on the righteous path where there are countless hills and valleys to explore
No need to worry, don't fret none, the Lord has equipped us to endure
Endure hardness as a good soldier of Jesus Christ.
No cares of this world can hinder you; you've got purpose and destiny to fulfill, fruit to spring forth, blossom and grow

Grow into the Masterpiece God has birthed within you to show…

Give God all the Glory that is due to only Him. You see when we surrender and walk completely in purpose you must win!

Purpose transforms you, it stretches you and sometimes it hurts. Purpose is a process – dare I say that word? Please do not view it as a curse.

We must see process and purpose through God's lens. We must be washed inside and out in order to be completely cleansed.

Purge me with hyssop, I cry out to God! Wash me within and without Lord, because you alone are God!

I AM WALKING IN PURPOSE; I HAVE NO DOUBT! MY MASTER, MY LOVE, MY STRENGTH CRIES OUT!
I HAVE PURPOSE TO FULFILL
IN YOU MY CHILD –
STAND UP, FOR YOU ARE NOT ALONE
YES, I HEAR EVERY GROAN.
BUT YOU MUST PUSH THROUGH
DON'T YOU SEE, I HAVE PLANS FOR YOU
TIME WILL REVEAL ALL FOR I AM REAL
Because PURPOSE RESIDES IN YOU

"HELP"

Lord, I need you now, please HELP ME JESUS RIGHT NOW!!!!!
I am crying out to YOU.
My family, my pastor nor first lady
of the church can do it…
No, none of them
ONLY YOU
I am calling on you Lord, please help me now. I am perplexed on every side; surely, I am going to die! If you do not step in and take control, I am going to lose it. I am going to go!
Deep into a spiraling black hole with no windows to jump out or into and no way of escape
Please help me Lord! I don't want to relate….
To the countless others who don't
have enough sense to repent.
I repent Lord, I repent, I come to you now.
On bended knee, Yes Lord, crawling to your bleeding side. I am turning from all wicked ways. I no longer serve the devil nor this wretched flesh. Please Lord, I have put them far away! I stomp on the enemy's head forever and ever, kill em dead! I never want to stay in the state of sin, separated from God and no hope to make it in.

I Love you TOO MUCH, I have longed my entire saved life to hold you near and hear those sweet words of comfort I pray.
Welcome my child into the kingdom. I love you. You obeyed.

"RISE UP LIONESS"

Come forth Lioness, we must hear your roar
You are BOLD, CONFIDENT,
FEARLESS and SELF ASSURED
Built up in the knowledge of God's character,
strength and truth,
You have nothing to fear, nor are you timid,
weak or afraid to move
My child, just look at the story of Ruth
No longer under the cloak of sin, death and the grave
The enemy must bow down and behave.
You are Alive! You are Free!
You have the authority to tell Satan,
get your hands off me!
He cannot touch thee!
You have the victory!
Rise up Lioness don't you see,
You will not be denied!
Rise up Lioness and claim your prize!

"AN ODE TO MY KING"

OH, MY MASTER AND KING, YOU ARE
WORTHY AND I BOW DOWN
TO YOU MY MAJESTY
HOLY AND AWESOME ARE WORDS TO
DESCRIBE YOUR MAGNIFICENCE
AND SPLENDOR
OH, HOLY ONE, WITH YOU
I LONG TO ABIDE
YOU ARE GOD, THE RULER OF ALL
WE LONG TO HEAR YOUR VOICE AND TO
YOU WE ALL BELONG
WE WERE DESIGNED TO WORSHIP,
ADORE AND MAGNIFY YOUR HOLY NAME
WE ARE YOURS OUR KING AND IN YOU
WE WISH TO REMAIN
KEEPER, STRENGTH, ROCK AND BALM
YOU ARE THE ONLY ONE
WHO KEEPS US CALM
JESUS YOU ARE LORD
THE ONE TRUE AND LIVING GOD
WE PRAY TO YOU MORNING,
NOON AND NIGHT
WE PRAY YOU FIND US WORTHY TO BE
YOUR BRIDE FOR THE REST OF OUR LIFE

HEAVEN AND EARTH,
WE TRUST AND OBEY
KEEP US LORD GOD FOR
THE REST OF OUR DAYS
WE LOVE YOU OUR KING
YOU ARE LOVE

www.ingramcontent.com/pod-product-compliance
Lightning Source LLC
Chambersburg PA
CBHW071325080526
44587CB00018B/3351